YORK NOTES

General Editors: Professor A.N. Jeffares (*University of Stirling*) & Professor Suheil Bushrui (*American University of Beirut*)

J. B. Priestley

AN INSPECTOR CALLS

Notes by Katie Gray
MA (OXFORD), MSC (EDINBURGH)

LONGMAN
YORK PRESS

YORK PRESS
Immeuble Esseily, Place Riad Solh, Beirut.

LONGMAN GROUP UK LIMITED
Longman House, Burnt Mill, Harlow,
Essex CM20 2JE, England
Associated companies, branches and representatives
throughout the world

First published 1990
Third impression 1992

ISBN 0-582-02095-6

Produced by Longman Group (FE) Ltd.
Printed in Hong Kong

Contents

Part 1

Introduction

Life of J. B. Priestley

John Boynton Priestley was born on 13 September 1894 in Bradford. He died nearly ninety years later on 14 August 1984 in Stratford-upon-Avon.

The son of a schoolmaster, he left school at sixteen and drifted into a job with a local wool merchant. He stayed in Bradford until the outbreak of World War I, eventually finding work on various local papers. He always remembered with great affection the Bradford of his youth with its closely knit society and its theatres. During the war he served in France (with a Yorkshire regiment, the 10th Duke of Wellington's), but he never made much of this experience in his writings, even though he was invalided home after being buried alive in the trenches. In 1919 he went to Trinity Hall, Cambridge, on an ex-serviceman's grant, and read Modern History and Political Science. He never really felt at home in Cambridge. He married an old Bradford girl-friend, Pat Tempest, in June 1921, and was determined to leave academic life as soon as possible. The offer of a job as University Extension Lecturer in North Devon did not appeal, so they moved to London where Priestley very soon began to make a living as a free-lance writer for newspapers and as a reader for Bodley Head, the publishers. The Priestleys' early married life was bohemian and relatively insecure until Priestley began to make a reputation for himself in the field of literary journalism, finally establishing himself after the publication of a much admired article on Thomas Love Peacock (1923) in *The Times Literary Supplement*. He also published a minor classic, *The English Comic Characters*, in 1925, the same year that his young wife died of cancer. Writing helped to distract him from his wife's prolonged illness; but he was also having and affair with Jane Wyndham Lewis and married her in 1926 after her divorce. The resultant family was a complicated one: there were Pat's children Barbara and Silvia, Jane's daughter from her first marriage Angela, and her baby daughter Mary who was actually Priestley's child, born while Pat was still alive. Priestley's second marriage was to last for twenty-six years, and although it began as a passionate love affair, the relationship was to be a tormented one, in part because of Priestley's affairs with other women.

By 1927 his writing career had taken off: he had already published five books of essays and five volumes of literary criticism, and his first novel was published that year; another twenty or so works of prose fiction were to follow. There were also eventually to be seven volumes of social history, seven volumes of semi-autobiography and travel, two of philosophical speculation and hundreds of articles and broadcasts. In 1929 the overwhelming success of the long picaresque novel *The Good Companions* made Priestley a national figure. The consequences of this overnight fame were not all beneficial, however. Certainly Priestley's financial position was now secure, and he was able to buy the first of a succession of large beautiful houses, an elegant Georgian house in Highgate, where Samuel Taylor Coleridge (1772–1834) had once lived. But his success was also in some way held against him; his critics never forgave him the vulgarity of having written a best-seller, and from now on his motives for writing were always taken to be financial ones. This was the beginning of his unceasing battle to be taken seriously by the critics, in which he was on the whole unsuccessful. Virginia Woolf (1882–1941), for instance, dismissed both Priestley and Arnold Bennett (1867–1931) as 'the tradesmen of letters'. Priestley's *Angel Pavement* (1930), a more serious, less romantic novel which evoked the social problems of the day and the fear of unemployment, was another thorough-going success. The 1930s too saw him attempting yet another kind of writing as he became increasingly involved with the theatre. His first play, *Dangerous Corner*, was first performed in 1932, although the production was only successful after Priestley himself provided substantial financial backing. It was to be succeeded by thirty-seven other plays. In 1934 he set out to visit the poorer parts of Britain, which he movingly described in *English Journey*, a supremely readable piece of popular sociology. These travels brought to the fore the political side of Priestley's nature which was to play an influential part in his public life and his writing.

These were by no means the only travels that Priestley undertook at this time. His wife's health required her to spend the winter months in a warm climate, so twice before 1937 the family visited America. Mrs Priestley and the children – there were six of them by now – settled in the Arizona desert, while Priestley himself went to New York to find a suitable American agent and to supervise the unsuccessful transfer of his first plays to Broadway, then to Hollywood, and then on an exhausting four-week lecture tour. Another winter was spent in Egypt and the Sudan. All this was useful material for his pen, as is testified by the numerous essays and autobiographical writings of the time, in particular *Midnight on the Desert* (1937).

The facility with which he wrote is legendary, and so is the fact that he never corrected the first draft of what he had written. There are many accounts of his regular writing habits, which were maintained in all circumstances (he even had a special hut built in Arizona to serve as his study) and which involved his turning his back on the view and plugging his ears with cotton-wool. This single-minded determination helps to explain how even during World War II he managed to write no fewer than fourteen books. During the war he also broadcast his sensitive and intuitive reflections, *Postscripts*, on Sunday evening radio. His delivery of these broadcasts was excellent due to his acting ability, and with their casual and colloquial style, they were much appreciated by listeners. However, some of Priestley's forthright criticisms of the government and his idealistically socialist views (after praising the Merchant Navy's heroism, for instance, he then pointed out how poorly the sailors were paid) eventually persuaded the BBC, on advice from the Ministry of Information, to withdraw the talks after a year. In fact Priestley's socialism was of the Keir Hardie brand (James Keir Hardie (1856–1915) was the founder of the Independent Labour Party). He did flirt with politics more than once and for a period seemed to become more and more left-wing in his views. He was chairman of the 1941 Committee (a left-wing group set up to prepare for the reform of society after the war), founded with Sir Richard Acland the Common Wealth Party (an alternative and radical new party), stood as an Independent candidate in Cambridge in 1944, and visited the Soviet Union in 1945. Yet by the 1950s he was expressing a hope for the return of the Liberals, and while he did become very involved in the Campaign for Nuclear Disarmament in its early stages, he backed out rather publicly when that movement seemed to be attracting radicals. He rightly described the basis for his politics as compassion, but the compassion was of a generalised nature and did not include a particularly coherent plan for reform. His play *They Came to a City* (1943), which uses the language of *Postscripts*, encapsulates his rather vague utopianism: nine characters, a rough cross-section of English society, are admitted to the city, a socialist dream world where justice, wealth and truth are equally distributed, and one of them is altruistic enough to return to the outside to tell the world of this new Jerusalem. Gradually, however, Priestley's compassion changed into a hectoring petulance against the Establishment, and nothing about the post-1914 world pleased him.

In 1930 Priestley came under the influence of *An Experiment with Time* (1927) by J. W. Dunne (1875–1949) and this, combined with his later reading of *A New Model of the Universe* (1931) by P. D. Ouspensky (1878–1947), and Dunne's second book, *The Serial*

Universe (1934), offered him an escape route away from the real world. He interpreted these three books rather idiosyncratically, and his confusing and confused ideas about time are treated in some detail in *Man and Time* (1964). From Dunne he takes the idea of a series of times that we can observe and dream of; and from Ouspensky a cyclical view of time in which events recur never-endingly, and only especially gifted people are able to intervene in this cyclical progress and change its course. Priestley uses these same ideas about time and dreams much more successfully in his plays. Sometimes the theme is overt and rather heavily handled as in *I Have Been Here Before* (1937), a play which took Priestley years rather than the customary week to write, probably because it was written to illustrate a theory. But the plays which deal with these theories more implicitly are among his most successful: *Dangerous Corner* (1932), *Eden End* (1934), *Time and the Conways* (1937) and *An Inspector Calls* (1945). Another result of Priestley's interest in time theories, combined with an avid reading of the Swiss psychoanalyst C. Jung (1875–1961), was his desire to experiment with dreams, allegory and parable in his plays, particularly in *Music at Night* (1937) and *Johnson over Jordan* (1939). *The Linden Tree*, staged in 1947, was Priestley's last successful production in the West End of London for some sixteen years.

During this same year Priestley embarked on a long and secret affair with the archaeologist Jacquetta Hawkes which began when they were both delegates to a UNESCO conference in Mexico City. Their marriage took place in 1953. There were echoes of the situation which had led up to his second marriage. Jacquetta Hawkes, like Jane Wyndham Lewis, had to obtain a divorce before she was in a position to marry Priestley. In 1954 he and his new wife moved from the previous Priestley home on the Isle of Wight to Stratford-upon-Avon. They collaborated on two plays and a travel book. This third marriage, which lasted thirty-one years, from Priestley's fifty-ninth year until his death, was an extremely happy one.

Priestley as a writer is very difficult to categorise as his literary output was so diverse and so prolific. He was an all-round man of letters and also a very competent musician and painter. In *Midnight on the Desert* (1937) he wrote:

> I have a restless nature, easily bored, and I flit from one kind of work to another, partly sustained by a very genuine interest in the technical problems of all forms of writing. I have always wanted vaguely to be an all-round man of letters on the eighteenth-century plan, which allowed or commanded a man to write an essay or poem, novel or play just as he pleased. (page 9)

His powerful personality is perhaps easier to define. He was an entertainer, a communicator, a moralist. He had great independence of mind and was innately romantic. His burly frame and his Yorkshire accent made him the epitome of the pipe-smoking Englishman, and in fact one of his nicknames was Jolly Jack. Blunt and brusque, he had the reputation of being downright difficult at times. He offers telling insights about himself in his many volumes of semi-discursive autobiographical writings, for example *Rain upon Godshill* (1939), *Thoughts in the Wilderness* (1957) and *Margin Released* (1962).

J. B. Priestley and the theatre

J. B. Priestley saw his novel-writing as a kind of journalism. Indeed the novels are often essays in disguise, and as such are particularly lacking in characterisation. He was much more naturally a playwright, although perhaps an old-fashioned one. His reputation as a dramatist was not confined to Britain: in 1945 after a tour of the Soviet Union he could say he was the most popular foreign author in Russia. His plays probably always enjoyed greater critical esteem abroad; at home he was too easily dismissed as 'middlebrow'. He resented this and saw it as his fate to have been born an extrovert in an age of introverts, when intensity was prized above creative energy.

After the success of *The Good Companions* (1929) and *Angel Pavement* (1930) Priestley's financial struggles to make a living were over and he accepted the challenge of writing plays, fully aware from the outset that his reputation in this field would be at the mercy of critics. He wrote for the stage from 1932 to 1963, and his theatrical output includes domestic dramas, modern moralities, plays on the philosophy of time, melodrama, farce and an adaptation of a contemporary novel. There was a revival of interest in his dramatic work in the 1970s, and his time plays were revived for his eightieth birthday in 1974. His first experience of working in the theatre was in collaboration with Edward Knoblock in dramatising his own *The Good Companions* (1929) for the New York stage, but he also had experience as director, critic and even briefly as an actor, in his own *When We Are Married* (1938). By the time *Dangerous Corner* (1932) was successfully staged he had become its manager in collaboration with his agent, A. D. Peters. He continued to be involved in management, underwriting plays at the Duchess and Westminster Theatres, and eventually founding the London Mask Theatre.

He wrote extensively if randomly about the theatre. In a talk reprinted in 1961 under the title 'What about the Audience?' he sees drama as still close to its original religious roots: 'something remains, to give a curious sense of urgency, a devotion to their duty, to all players, directors, writers who have not lost the last whisper of conscience'. Mostly, however, he was specifically interested in the theatre as seen from the writer's point of view. In his lecture 'The Art of the Dramatist' (1957) he sees the pre-eminence of the dramatist over the actor and the director as vital for a healthy theatre. He maintains that good drama has to work on two levels, combining on the one hand realistic characters and actions, with, on the other, the highly conventional art of the theatre. In *Theatre Outlook* (1947) he lays great emphasis on production and staging: 'In a good theatrical production we are offered a piece of life so shaped and coloured and contrived that everything in it, down to the smallest detail, is significant' (page 71). He explains in detail his methods for heightening reality in the Introduction to the first volume of his *Collected Plays* (Heinemann, London, 1945): he admits to trying to conjure audiences away from reality after persuading them for the first half-hour that they are within its bounds; this explains why he favours a play in one set. He can start 'in a sensible and respectable sitting room' and then begin playing his tricks and 'edging away from conventional realism' (page viii).

Although now, with the exception of *An Inspector Calls* (written in the winter of 1944 and first published in 1945), Priestley's plays tend to be taken up enthusiastically by amateurs rather than performed on the professional stage, during the 1930s and 1940s he overshadowed his contemporaries Noel Coward (1899–1973), W. S. Maugham (1874–1965) and Sean O'Casey (1884–1964). The influence he admitted to was that of Anton Chekhov (1860–1904) whom he much admired and some of whose plays he saw performed by the Moscow Art Theatre. T. S. Eliot (1888–1965) and W. B. Yeats (1865–1939), on the other hand, he condemned for their overly poetic approach to drama. 'The closely ordered modern prose drama, tied to probability and realistic behaviour, cannot achieve the wild and startling beauty of great poetic drama, but its very construction, to an alert mind can bring intellectual delight' ('The Art of the Dramatist', page 28).

Vincent Brome in his recent biography of Priestley sums up the critical reputation of his plays while refusing to decide whether he was a better playwright than a novelist:

Theatrically he took risks, he married the unmarriageable, he experimented with what were then fashionable theories of time, which invited disaster. He could fall over into sentimentality and sometimes his dialogue which set out to heighten common speech merely reported it, but he remained a very effective playwright who reflected life in multi-faceted detail and entertained millions throughout the world.

A note on the text

The most readily available text of *An Inspector Calls* is the one published by Heinemann Educational Books in the Hereford Plays series. This edition was originally published in 1965 but has been reprinted every year since then – which is one obvious sign of the popularity of the play. It has an introduction and detailed questions on the text, and is the text referred to in these Notes. There is also an acting edition published by Samuel French, London (1948).

An Inspector Calls was first produced in Moscow in 1945. Critics claimed later that the play had been rejected by various London managements, but according to Priestley it was simply a matter of the unavailability of a suitable theatre which persuaded him to send a copy of the script to Moscow. Its first production in London was on 1 October 1946 at the New Theatre, London, with a cast which included Alec Guinness and Ralph Richardson. Since then it has been staged repeatedly in Britain and around the world. In 1953 there was a film version starring Alastair Sim. The play has also been shown on BBC television, and was revived in London in 1974 and 1987.

Part 2

Summaries
of AN INSPECTOR CALLS

A general summary

Act 1

The scene is a prosperous Edwardian dining-room. Mr and Mrs Birling, their children Sheila and Eric, and Gerald Croft have just had dinner together to celebrate Gerald's engagement to Sheila. They are feeling very pleased with themselves, and Mr Birling has just finished making a pompous speech when a police inspector arrives. He tells them that he is making enquiries about a girl who has committed suicide. At first Mr Birling tries to send him away, but, on being shown a photograph of her, has to admit that he did know the dead girl, and had sacked her after a strike. Then Sheila is shown the photograph and confesses that she made the girl lose her next job through jealousy and petty-mindedness. By the end of the act Gerald too is clearly involved.

From the start Eric and Sheila have been more easily moved and prepared to accept some responsibility for the girl's death. Gerald on the other hand has sided with the parents in refusing to acknowledge any involvement in the event. Already there appears to be something odd about the Inspector.

Act 2

In this act it is Mrs Birling who makes the overly self-assured remarks and tries to frighten the Inspector away. Gerald admits to having picked up the girl the previous spring. She became his mistress and he kept her for a few months until it no longer suited him. Sheila listens to these confessions from her fiancé and eventually comes to admire him, at least for his honesty. Sheila has already sensed that Mrs Birling is soon to be implicated too and has tried to prevent her from insisting too hard that her values are the right ones. In fact Mrs Birling is eventually made to admit that two weeks previously she had refused financial help to the girl who was by then pregnant. It becomes clear that the father was probably Eric.

Act 3

Eric confesses to having got the girl pregnant while he was drunk. Then as she refused to marry him, he used money that he had obtained by fraud from his father's business to keep her. The Birling family unity begins to disintegrate in self-accusatory arguments. They are by now to some extent prepared to accept their part in the girl's death. The Inspector gives them a final, moralising talk about mutual responsibility and leaves. Gerald helps to convince Mr and Mrs Birling that the Inspector was not a real inspector, that they have all been talking about different girls, that probably there was not even a dead body. Sheila and Eric resist this strongly, even when the Infirmary denies that any girl died there that night. They feel that the experience has changed them, even if the Inspector was not all he seemed. Then, however, the phone rings. Mr Birling answers, to be told by the police at the other end that a girl has died on her way to the Infirmary and that an inspector will call to make enquiries.

Detailed summaries

As there are no scene divisions, the exits and entrances of the main characters will be used to divide the three acts into convenient sections for study purposes.

The page references are to the Heinemann edition.

ACT 1

Page 1

Act 1 begins with detailed and practical stage directions. We are in the large suburban house of a prosperous manufacturer. The four members of the Birling family and their guest are briefly described. They are at the end of a celebratory meal and are all pleased with themselves.

Pages 2–7 (Birling: Giving us the port, Edna? . . . Birling and Gerald sit down again.)

The port is passed round. They all fill their glasses and prepare to toast Sheila and Gerald on their engagement. Very quickly the banter between them establishes the characters as the stage directions describe them: we soon notice Birling's easy manner and provincial speech, his wife's coldness and social superiority, Sheila's youthful excitedness and Eric's mixture of shyness and assertiveness. Gerald Croft stands out as the well-bred man-about-town. Birling makes a speech in which he congratulates the engaged pair and looks forward to a closer business collaboration with Gerald's father who, we gather, is abroad. They drink. Gerald presents Sheila with a ring. Birling continues his speech; he wants them to be very confident about the future. (Remember the play was written in 1944, but is set in 1912, so this is a way of suggesting Birling's insensitivity.) He assures them that there will be peace and prosperity and rapid progress everywhere, and that the rumours of war are totally unfounded. Sheila and Mrs Birling get up to leave the gentlemen to their port. They take Eric with them.

NOTES AND GLOSSARY:

I'll ring from the drawing-room: at the end of a formal dinner the men would stay drinking at the table and the women would 'withdraw' to the drawing-room where coffee was served later

Arthur, you're not supposed to say such things: Mrs Birling does not like her husband to be too informal and familiar

except for all last summer: we shall eventually discover what Gerald was actually doing during the summer

squiffy: (*colloquial*) period word for 'drunk'

Chump: affectionate way of saying 'idiot'

Steady the Buffs: Eric is teasing his sister because she is kissing her fiancé, and tells the two of them to hold back. 'Steady the Buffs' is a phrase of admonition or encouragement, based on an incident in the history of the East Kent Regiment, nicknamed the Buffs

the Kaiser: the German Emperor Wilhelm II (reigned 1888–1918)

fiddlesticks: nonsense

the Balkans: countries of the Balkan peninsula in south-eastern Europe. They comprise Yugoslavia, Greece, Albania, Bulgaria and Rumania

the *Titanic*: the famous liner, which of course sank on her maiden voyage which Birling mentions. The whole of his speech is studded with references to a future of peace and progress, while the audience from their perspective know that this is a false prophecy and that two world wars will follow

these Bernard Shaws and H. G. Wellses: George Bernard Shaw
(1856–1950), an Irish dramatist and critic who was
an active socialist, and H. G. Wells (1866–1946), a
novelist who dealt with contemporary social
questions in *Kipps* (1905)

Pages 7–9 (Birling: Cigar? . . . Eric enters.)

Birling, now alone with Gerald, brings the talk round to Gerald's
mother, Lady Croft, who seems to think that her son is marrying
beneath his station. Birling mentions the strong possibility of his soon
becoming Sir Arthur Birling (Gerald's father is Sir George Croft).
Eric enters.

NOTES AND GLOSSARY:
old county family – landed people: Lady Croft's family has been part
of the land-owning aristocracy for centuries
Honours List: twice a year the Monarch (on advice from the
Prime Minister) draws up a list of people who are
to be rewarded for their services to the country by
being given a title or other honour
knighthood: honour which carries the title of Sir. (Priestley
himself refused both a knighthood and peerage.
In 1977 he was awarded the Order of Merit)
Lord Mayor: the head of the corporation of a large city
we'll try to keep out of trouble: in view of what is just about to happen
to the family this is an ironic comment

Pages 9–11 (Eric: What's the joke? . . . Inspector Goole.)

Eric enters, tells Birling and Gerald not to be too long over their
drinks and reports on the fact that his mother and sister are as ever
talking about clothes. Birling lectures the two young men again and
tells them to make their own way in the world, without depending on
anyone – at which point the doorbell rings. An Inspector Goole is
announced.

NOTES AND GLOSSARY:
I remember – (*but he checks himself*): Eric does have something to
hide
fishy: (*colloquial*) suspicious
the way some of these cranks talk and write now: Shaw and Wells
have already been mentioned. Birling is opposed
to all socialist views

crank: eccentric person who stubbornly maintains unusual views

a man has to mind his own business and look after himself and his own: the validity of this attitude is going to be disproved by the play

Give us some more light: see the stage directions on page 1. The lighting is to change from intimate to bright and hard when the Inspector enters

And that would be awkward: they will not be able to joke for long

---

Pages 11–16 (The Inspector enters . . . Sheila has now entered.)

The stage directions describe the Inspector: he is solid and purposeful and looks hard at the person he is speaking to. He brusquely tells the three men that a young girl has just committed suicide by drinking disinfectant and that a reading of her diary has brought him to this house. Birling, assuming that he can handle the Inspector, starts off impatiently, expressing his puzzlement at how he might be involved. However, prompted by a name and a photograph, he remembers that the girl had been an employee of his and that he had sacked her. Gerald wonders if, out of politeness, he should go, but the Inspector detains him; he also emphasises that the involvement of any one of them with the girl might establish a chain of events leading to her suicide. We then hear more details about Birling's connection with the girl, Eva Smith. She was involved in a strike for higher wages, which failed, and lost her job because she was one of the ring-leaders.

Eric comments rather naïvely on the unfairness of employers always looking for higher prices while their employees cannot ask for higher wages. Birling and Gerald as hard businessmen make fun of this attitude, but Eric cannot see why the girl could not have been kept on as she was a good worker. Sheila enters at this point.

NOTES AND GLOSSARY:

alderman: senior member of the corporation of a city

on the Bench: serving as a magistrate

Brumley: the industrial town in which the play is set

Infirmary: hospital

Any particular reason why I shouldn't see this girl's photograph: the Inspector is very careful to let only one person at a time see the photograph of the girl

early autumn of nineteen-ten: a reminder of the period in which the play is set and of the length of the family's involvement with the girl

obviously it was nothing whatever to do with the wretched girl's suicide: Birling is clearly on the wrong track here

I can't accept any responsibility: Birling begins to repeat the views expressed in his earlier speech to Gerald and Eric. He is going to learn that he must change his attitude

Why?: this strange question makes Birling realise that there is definitely something odd about the Inspector

go on the streets: become a prostitute

Pages 17–21 (Sheila (gaily): What's this about streets? . . . The other three stare in amazement for a moment.)

Sheila, coming to fetch the men to the drawing-room, interrupts the conversation. Birling is unwilling for her to be involved, but she is moved by the description of the girl's death, and the Inspector insists on her staying. He then goes on to imply that they all share involvement in the girl's death. He also tells them that after leaving the factory Eva Smith changed her name and went to work in a local dress-shop where again she was commended for her work, but was dismissed because a customer complained about her attitude. Sheila becomes agitated, asks to see the photograph and then runs out.

NOTES AND GLOSSARY:

It's a rotten shame: Sheila is moved not only by the suicide, but by the account of the girl's poverty after she had lost her first job

Ask your father: the Inspector is emphasising Birling's hard business attitudes

these girls aren't cheap labour: Sheila on the other hand reacts with humanity

dingy: dirty-looking

short-handed: without enough shop-assistants

At the end of January – last year: gradually we are learning about the girl's life up to her suicide

---

Page 21 (Birling: What's the matter with her? . . . The Inspector ignores them.)

As Sheila rushes out Birling turns on the Inspector for upsetting her, and then goes out to speak to his wife.

NOTES AND GLOSSARY:
a nasty mess somebody's made of it: the Inspector's moralising tone becomes steadily stronger

---

Pages 21–22 (Gerald: I'd like to have a look at that photograph . . . who looks as if she's been crying.)

Gerald, Eric and the Inspector await Sheila's return. The Inspector will not let Gerald see the photograph yet. Sheila comes in looking as if she had been crying.

NOTES AND GLOSSARY:
if it was left to me: the Inspector is moralising again

Pages 22–25 (Well, Miss Birling? . . . then goes out with Eric.)

Sheila comes in to make her confession. She admits that she had the girl sacked out of sheer bad temper. When the girl looked better in a dress than she did herself, Sheila was very jealous and reported her to the manager for impertinence. The Inspector makes her realise just how shocking her behaviour was. He then sums up what he has uncovered so far and tells them that the girl now changed her name to Daisy Renton. Gerald is startled. The Inspector goes out with Eric to fetch Birling, leaving Sheila and Gerald alone.

NOTES AND GLOSSARY:
rotten: guilty
you're partly to blame: the Inspector's mission is to get them all to share responsibility
I'm trying to tell the truth: Sheila is to be admired for her openness and readiness to accept the blame and to feel guilty
It's too late: the Inspector deals very harshly with anyone who belatedly wishes things had been different
it's a bit thick: (*colloquial*) it's rather shocking
tantalus: case in which bottles may be locked with their contents tantalisingly visible

---

Pages 25–26 (Well, Gerald? . . . Inspector: Well?)

Sheila has suddenly understood what Gerald was doing last summer: having an affair with Daisy Renton. Gerald tries to pretend differently, but Sheila has already passed beyond such small-mindedness. The Inspector returns.

NOTES AND GLOSSARY:
Why – you fool – *he knows*: Sheila has understood the Inspector's role as an outside agent who will make them reveal all

ACT 2
The scene and the situation are exactly the same as at the end of Act 1.

Pages 27–32 (At rise, scene and situation are exactly . . . Enter Birling, who closes door behind him.)

Gerald tries to persuade Sheila to leave before he makes his confession. Sheila and the Inspector decide she should stay. Gerald is very bitter, and accuses her of wanting to see him shamed in the same way as she has been. They begin to quarrel. The Inspector takes charge and expresses Sheila's feelings very forcibly: she has understood her part in the girl's death but she needs to stay and hear that she is not solely responsible. Mrs Birling comes in, striking quite the wrong note. Sheila senses this and tries to stop her mother being so superior and confident. She attempts to stop her mother creating a wall between herself and the girl because she knows the Inspector will break it down. Mrs Birling is still offended by the Inspector. Gerald joins with Sheila in trying to stop Mrs Birling. Eric's drinking is discussed, and much to Mrs Birling's surprise both Sheila and Gerald confirm that he has been drinking too much for the past two years. Mr Birling, who has been trying to persuade Eric to go to bed, comes in.

NOTES AND GLOSSARY:
we'll have to share our guilt: the Inspector shows an uncanny ability to understand Sheila's feelings
They're more impressionable: indeed Sheila and Eric have been more easily moved by the girl's fate, and certainly Sheila has been ready to accept her part in the girl's death
offence: a play on words: to take offence, to be offended, and to commit an offence, to break a law
Isn't he used to drinking?: we have already seen that Eric drinks too much. Part of Mrs Birling's 'wall' is that she cannot admit such things
This isn't the time to pretend: Sheila knows that they must all be totally honest in front of the Inspector

Pages 32–40 (Birling (rather hot, bothered): I've been trying to persuade Eric . . . Gerald: I don't think so. Excuse me.)

Birling comes in, saying that Eric should go to bed. The Inspector says that he told Eric to stay up and wait his turn. Mr and Mrs Birling express their resentment at the way the Inspector is treating them. The Inspector turns to Gerald and asks him when he first met the girl (who took the name Daisy Renton after she had to leave the shop). Gerald admits to having met her in a bar and having noticed that she was different from the other women there. She was being molested by a local dignitary, and Gerald managed to send him away and rescue the girl by taking her to a hotel. They talked. She was deliberately vague about her past life, but clearly poor and hungry. Gradually Gerald became involved: he arranged to meet her again, found rooms for her and eventually she became his mistress.

Birling objects to Sheila having to hear all this, but he is overruled. Gerald explains that he was not really in love with her, but that he enjoyed the situation. He broke off the relationship when he had to go away in September but gave the girl some money to live on. The Inspector continues the story from the girl's diary: she went away for a couple of months to treasure the memory of the affair. Sheila has come to respect Gerald on hearing his confession because he has been totally honest. Nevertheless she hands him back his ring because she feels that now they will have to get to know each other again. The Inspector allows Gerald to go out for a walk.

NOTES AND GLOSSARY:

You needn't give me any rope: to give somebody rope (to hang himself) means to allow him the freedom to bring about his own discomfiture. Sheila has rightly understood that it is the Inspector who is giving them rope

Daisy Renton, with other ideas: given that the play is set in 1912 the fact that Daisy Renton became a prostitute has to be expressed in euphemistic language

the stalls bar at the Palace: the bar on the ground floor at a variety theatre – so the clientele would be fairly low-class

you're obviously going to hate this: Gerald is understandably made tense by Sheila's presence

haunt of women of the town: a favourite place for prostitutes to congregate

you're forgetting I'm supposed to be engaged to the hero of it: Sheila has to be very sarcastic in order to cope with the situation

dough-faced women: we already know that Daisy Renton was pretty, not like the other women with their flabby faces

goggle-eyed: with eyes popping out of his head

obscene fat carcase: Gerald uses particularly strong language as he remembers the scene

womanizer . . . one of the worst sots: a man who chases women and drinks too much

we *are* learning something: Mrs Birling is still trying to distance herself from the story as it unfolds. She also unwittingly shows that other supposedly respectable people behaved badly towards Daisy Renton

let slip: reveal

(*steadily*): the stage directions point out the straightforward way in which Gerald makes his difficult confession

Somehow he makes you: Sheila and Gerald realise the Inspector's power at extracting these honest confessions from them

Your daughter isn't living on the moon: the Inspector resists any attempt to protect Sheila from the unpleasant aspects of life such as Daisy Renton had to face

At least it's honest: Sheila is coming to admire Gerald

first week of September: gradually the chronology of Daisy Renton's last months is being pieced together. This is the purpose of the Inspector's inquiry

a rough sort of a diary: this is the convenient back-up for the Inspector's story

(*She hands him the ring*): Sheila feels she can no longer be engaged to Gerald, although, ironically, she respects him more than she used to

---

Pages 40–42 (He goes out . . . Birling: I'll see.)

Sheila comments on the fact that Gerald did not see the photograph. It is now shown to Mrs Birling who pretends she does not recognise the girl in it. The Inspector tells her she is lying; Mr Birling is offended. Sheila tries to persuade her mother that she must be honest. The door slams again. Mr Birling goes to investigate.

NOTES AND GLOSSARY:

you weren't asked to come here to talk to me about my responsibilities: Sheila sees beyond this and recognises the prophetic nature of the Inspector's presence

---

Page 42 (He goes out quickly . . . Enter Birling, looking rather agitated.)

The Inspector starts questioning Mrs Birling, reminding her that two weeks ago she chaired the meeting of an organisation for helping women in trouble. Mr Birling comes in; it appears that Eric has gone out.

NOTES AND GLOSSARY:

in helping deserving cases: in helping only those cases which appeal to Mrs Birling's patronising sense of charity

---

Pages 42–49 (Birling: That must have been Eric . . . Curtain falls quickly.)

Mr Birling and Sheila are amazed to learn that Mrs Birling saw the girl two weeks previously, when she came for financial help. Mrs Birling aggressively excuses herself from any blame, revealing her snobbishness and prejudice and her lack of sympathy. She did not like the girl's manner, she did not believe the girl's story, so she used her influence with her committee to see that the girl was refused any money. She sees herself as having done her duty.

The Inspector reveals that the girl was pregnant and that Mrs Birling knew this. Mrs Birling claims that the father should have helped, but the Inspector quickly manages to make Sheila (because she is sensitive) and Birling (because he is worried about his position) feel that this attitude is wrong. Mrs Birling's next defence is that the girl knew who the father was and was giving herself airs by pretending to have scruples about where he was getting the money he was giving her.

The Inspector cuts through all her protestations and forces her to admit that the girl thought the money had been stolen. The Inspector tries to make her sorry for the girl's death, but Mrs Birling continues to insist that it was the girl's fault and that the father was the chief culprit. Sheila sees what is coming and tries to stop her mother. Mrs Birling elaborates on how, if the father were caught, he should be made to admit his guilt publicly. Too late she realises that Eric is probably the father. Eric comes in.

NOTES AND GLOSSARY:

only two weeks ago: the jigsaw is nearly complete
she called herself Mrs Birling: we learn later why
she had only herself to blame: like her husband Mrs Birling does not believe in sharing responsibility

I didn't like her manner: in the past this was also Sheila's and Mr Birling's attitude. And because of their social position they could squash the girl

Unlike the other three, I did nothing I'm ashamed of: she is wrong and the Inspector tells her so

The Press might easily take it up: Mr Birling begins to be seriously worried about his knighthood

absurd in a girl in her position: Mrs Birling has a very hierarchical view of society

the father was only a youngster – silly and wild and drinking too much: a description of Eric for us to take note of

He should be made an example of: Mrs Birling is going to be caught in her own trap

No hushing up: no hiding the truth. This is exactly what the Inspector wants

ACT 3
The scene and the situation are exactly the same as at the end of Act 2.

Pages 50–52 (Exactly as at end of Act Two . . . Then he closes it and comes in.)

Eric comes back and soon realises that Mrs Birling and Sheila have well and truly compromised him. He needs a drink, which the Inspector allows him, then he begins his confession: he was drunk in the Palace bar and picked up Daisy Renton and insisted on going home with her and making love to her. At this point Birling insists that Sheila take her mother out of the room.

NOTES AND GLOSSARY:

You don't know what we've been saying: from a dramatic point of view we need to know the details of Eric's relationship with the girl, even though Eric is not yet aware of his mother's part

sneak: tale-teller

There'll be plenty of time, when I've gone: we are getting to the end of the play. The Inspector will soon leave them to reflect on their shared responsibility for the girl's death

last November: two months after the girl's affair with Gerald

In the Palace bar: the same bar where Gerald met her

I was rather far gone: I was very drunk

And that's when it happened: more euphemisms

Pages 52–53 (Inspector: When did you meet her again? . . . Mrs Birling and Sheila come back.)

Eric continues his story: he met Daisy again, made love to her again. Then he learnt she was pregnant. She treated him like a child: refused to marry him, refused to live off stolen money. Mr Birling is just about to ascertain where Eric's first stolen fifty pounds came from, when his wife and daughter come back.

NOTES AND GLOSSARY:
a good sport: an agreeable, easy-going person
fat old tarts: prostitutes

Pages 53–56 (Sheila: This isn't my fault . . . Good night.)

Mrs Birling and Sheila cannot stay away: this is an excuse for Mr Birling to recapitulate Eric's story. Eric goes on to explain how he managed to defraud the firm and how he hoped to pay the money back. He is taken aback to learn that the Inspector already knows that the girl would not take his stolen money. His mother's part in the story is revealed to him. His reaction is a very emotional one: he accuses his mother of killing her own grandchild. The Inspector takes charge. He has come to the end of his inquiry; he reminds each of them in turn of their involvement. He has a kind word for Gerald (who has not yet returned) who at least made the girl happy for a time. The Inspector's tone becomes apocalyptic as he makes his final speech, and he then departs.

NOTES AND GLOSSARY:
cover this up: stop this becoming known
why didn't you come to me: if nothing else the Inspector's visit has made the gap between parents and children explicit
You don't understand anything: having just accused his father of not understanding him, he now accuses his mother of the same failing
they will be taught it in fire and blood and anguish: the Inspector's final words, which reveal him to be not just an inspector but the agent of some moral force

---

Pages 56–61 (He walks straight out . . . It's Mr Croft.)

Mr Birling immediately turns on Eric and blames him for everything. He is very worried about a public scandal because he does not want to lose his chance of a knighthood. As Sheila points out, Mr and Mrs Birling quickly revert to their old way of thinking, as if nothing had happened. Eric bitterly recalls that before the Inspector walked in Mr Birling was arguing that people should look after themselves and that one should not listen to cranks who said otherwise. Sheila realises that the Inspector's arrival was almost too opportune. She reveals that she has always had her doubts about him: was he really an inspector?

Mr and Mrs Birling seize on this; Sheila and Eric maintain it makes no difference, but Mr and Mrs Birling start to list all the ways in which the Inspector seemed unlike an ordinary policeman. As they wonder what to do next Gerald comes back.

NOTES AND GLOSSARY:

But don't forget I'm ashamed of you as well: Eric feels that they are now all equal because they all share the responsibility for the girl's death

There's every excuse: Mr Birling on the other hand believes that only Eric is responsible

you don't seem to have learnt anything: Sheila is not referring to actions and events but to the fact that her parents have not changed their whole attitude to the world while she and Eric have

He was our police inspector all right: Eric feels, like Sheila, that they have all had to face questions which forced them to think about their responsibilities; to that extent it does not matter if the person who questioned them was was a real inspector or not

inquest: official inquiry into a death

We hardly ever told him anything he didn't know: yet another instance of the Inspector's almost superhuman nature

bluffed: deceived

you allowed yourselves to be bluffed: Birling already sees their confessions to the Inspector as some kind of weakness

Probably a Socialist or some sort of crank: as we have seen, Birling dismisses people with humanitarian feelings as political radicals

---

Pages 61–72 (Gerald appears . . . the curtain falls.)

Gerald comes back. While he was out he made inquiries about Inspector Goole. There is no such person. Mr Birling phones the Chief Constable who confirms this. Mr and Mrs Birling begin to relax, and with Gerald they start to work out exactly how they have been tricked. Eric and Sheila are upset and angry as they see the other three beginning to act as if nothing had happened. The two of them cannot forget that a girl has died and they were involved in her death. Mr Birling comes down very strongly on Eric: as far as he is concerned stealing money from the firm is a much worse crime. Gerald interrupts and helps them all see that even though they were each guilty of some cruelty to a girl, it was not necessarily the same girl: for a start the photographs could all have been of different girls. Then he goes further and wonders if there was even a dead body: perhaps the Inspector just needed to shock them all at the beginning. Gerald phones the Infirmary and learns that indeed nobody has been brought in after drinking disinfectant.

Mr and Mrs Birling and Gerald are triumphant. They pour themselves a drink. Sheila and Eric are still upset. For them things have not returned to the way they were before; they feel they have learnt something. As Gerald tries to persuade Sheila to take back her ring the telephone rings: Mr Birling answers and is told that an inspector is on his way to make inquiries about a suicide.

NOTES AND GLOSSARY:

force: the police force

By Jingo: expression of surprise

We've been had: we've been tricked

I suppose we're all nice people now: Sheila refuses to forget what she has learnt about herself

a hoax: a trick

There were probably four or five different girls: one that Mr Birling sacked, one that Sheila had sacked, one with whom Gerald had an affair, and then probably the girl whom Eric got pregnant and who then was refused money by Mrs Birling

one of our employees: Gerald is just pretending, in order to have a reason to make his enquiry at all

moonshine: foolish talk, nonsense

an elaborate sell: a complicated confidence trick

But it might have done: Sheila is still not persuaded that anything has really changed

a police inspector is on his way here – to ask some – questions: the audience is left to wonder how the course of events is likely to be different this time round

Part 3

Commentary

Reading a play

Reading a play is very different from reading a novel. The author's intention in writing the play has been to see it performed on the stage, and to that extent the words in front of you are not the finished product, but rather a guide to the finished product. The theatrical performance is what you have to try and imagine as you read. It is this which gives rise to the possibilities of different interpretations and different productions of the same play. You become involved in a closed circle: as the characters begin to come alive for you, you begin to give a particular meaning to the words that they say. It can sometimes come as a shock to see or hear an alternative version which has taken a different view of the same characters. The richness of a play can be partly judged by the variety of interpretations that it yields. Shakespeare's plays are a case in point.

You need to exercise your imagination in order to decide what the characters and the setting look like, and also how the characters move and react to the plot as it unfolds. Do not skip the stage directions, because they are your most useful clue as to how you should visualise the characters. You need them too to help you imagine stage details, like the lighting, the position of each of the characters on the stage as the curtain goes up, and so on. As it becomes necessary in the course of the play, bracketed instructions tell you about the entrances and exits of all the characters, and also about any important actions they take or gestures they make (for example, Eric helping himself to a drink, or Sheila admiring her ring).

You also have to exercise your aural imagination. The occasional authorial comments in brackets are useful here. Priestley is helping you to understand the characters by giving you hints as to how they speak his words. Indeed you will notice that many of these comments are adverbs like 'imperturbably', 'grandly', 'apologetically'. These, however, are the only descriptive insights you get from the author. The rest you have to gain from the words of his characters. The best way of doing that is probably to read the play aloud with others.

It is important to bear in mind the year in which the play is set: 1912. This is at the end of the Edwardian period, a period of relative economic and social stability before the outbreak of World War I. The Birlings' life-style as reflected in their dining-room (the only room that we see in the course of the play) is elegant and very luxurious. You must keep in mind how the Inspector stands out as someone from a different world: he is dressed more simply, so he looks different; he defies the social conventions of the time, so he behaves differently; his speech rhythms are different, so he sounds different.

Technical considerations

In many ways *An Inspector Calls* is a perfect play. It contains theatrical excitement in the thriller-like suspense of the Inspector's inquiry; it has a moral message; it is very tightly constructed. At the same time it foils the audience's expectations of a conventional plot: the Inspector is not what he seems and he has not come to find out any facts: he already knows them.

The play was written in a week. As Priestley says in the Introduction to Volume 3 of his *Collected Plays* (1950) which includes *An Inspector Calls*: 'Plays of this kind, in which one situation inevitably leads to another, and in which a certain uniformity of manner and tone are essential, are in my view best written quickly' (page vi). It is obvious from the first page that J. B. Priestley is a skilful technician; the stage directions go halfway to meet the producers by suggesting ways in which the set and the placing of the dining-table can be dealt with. The handling of the photograph, so that it is only seen by one person at a time, is another example of Priestley's theatrical technique.

The action is continuous through the three acts, and we never leave the dining-room. There is therefore a tight unity of time and place, and Priestley's manipulation of his characters' exits and entrances becomes crucial. Each one of them is always provided with a convincing reason for leaving the stage, and the plot always exploits these temporary absences. Each act ends on a moment of tension, with a final entrance which, while not necessarily dramatic in itself, leads the audience on to an excited expectation of what will happen next. For instance, Eric conveniently goes for a walk while his mother comes to realise that he must have made Daisy Renton pregnant; Act 3 can therefore begin with his return to the dining-room to be confronted by his parents. The climax in this act comes with the Inspector's almost biblical summing-up, but the play does not end there. Nor does it end with the final curtain, as Priestley manages to sustain suspense beyond the last words of his play. The plot itself is carefully handled. It consists basically of the Inspector's almost inquisitorial attempt to reconstruct the last two years of the life of Eva Smith, alias Daisy Renton. This involves his compelling all five characters to admit in turn the part each played in her death. The audience has the chance to anticipate the plot and there are pointers throughout to what is about to happen. The audience also knows what happened after the period in which the play is set, and this helps to create an atmosphere of ironic tension.

Genre

What category of drama does the play fall into? This is surprisingly difficult to establish. *An Inspector Calls* has the pattern of a comedy in so far as the interest is divided equally between all the characters, and it begins with an engagement like a social comedy. But the comedy is reversed as soon as Eva Smith's death is announced; in fact the Inspector almost revels in frequently reminding the elegant diners of the gruesomeness of her suicide. The play becomes the tragedy of the girl who is not there, the protagonist who is off stage, yet whose death links all the living characters together, and postpones the impending marriage. Again *An Inspector Calls* is not a real detective story (a 'whodunnit') either. There is a detective of sorts and a body which we never see. But the Inspector knows from the beginning who is guilty, of what, when and where. His job is to induce the characters to admit their guilt. In fact the suspense lessens as the play develops because the audience begins to be able to anticipate the action, through the symmetry of the plot.

An Inspector Calls, however, fits into the dramatic convention of realistic plays as developed in Europe in the late nineteenth and early twentieth centuries – for instance, *Hedda Gabler* (1890) by Henrik Ibsen (1828–1906), or Shaw's *Heartbreak House* (1919). This kind of play is typically concerned with showing that behind the veneer of middle-class society there are truths which society finds difficult to accept. Many of Priestley's plays make their political point in this way. *An Inspector Calls* reveals the double standards by which the Birlings and their like can get away with behaving badly while the 'lower classes', represented by Eva Smith/Daisy Renton, cannot succeed in life even when they are hard-working and honest. *An Inspector Calls* is also quite deliberately a 'period piece', set thirty years before the time it was written. We never leave the Edwardian period dining-room; we, the audience, look in and observe characters getting on with their enclosed lives. In addition it is within the tradition of the well-made play with a neat, interlocking, symmetrical plot which allows the audience to trace with exactitude the pattern of the confessions that the Inspector will extract.

Language

Just as *An Inspector Calls* harks back to the nineteenth-century tradition of naturalism for its genre it does so for its use of language as well. In fact even Priestley's play-writing experiments never involved experimentation in language, although they presented challenges to the producer and stage designer with their large casts and multi-media effects. There are no modernist verbal innovations, and the language is usually one-dimensional and lacking in individuality, and thus more likely to establish tone than character. The characters' speech is presented as being realistic, although not until later in the century do we find playwrights like Harold Pinter (*b.* 1930) trying to imitate the linguistic muddle of real-life speech.

The most distinctive voice in *An Inspector Calls* is that of the Inspector himself. As the focal point of the play, he speaks 'carefully' and 'weightily', and since his role is to develop the plot, he controls the conversation and his speech is filled with questions and imperatives. As controller he interrupts anything that distracts from the direction he wants his inquiry to take; he also keeps reminding the five characters of the horrors of the night. He is at odds with them linguistically. The atmosphere that the realistic nature of the family's speech creates changes when the Inspector enters. It is not just his physical appearance and manner that are different, but the rhythms of his speech as well. There is a curious blend of the matter-of-fact and the rhetorical in the manner in which he speaks; he sometimes uses long sentences to emphasise what he is saying, breaking them up into strong, rhythmic phrases ('And if she leaves us now, and doesn't hear any more, then she'll feel she's entirely to blame, she'll be alone with her responsibility, the rest of tonight, all tomorrow, all the next night –' [Act 2]). This contrasts so strongly with initial audience expectations of the Inspector and with the way the other characters speak that a very particular atmosphere is created – a strange mixture of the realistic and the almost mystical. The audience thus becomes aware very early on that they are being presented with rather more than a straightforward naturalistic drama.

Priestley has several possibilities open to him to vary the way his characters interact: monologues, dialogues, everyone talking at once. Most of the language of the play is in the form of lively conversation. This close-knit group of people whose defences are down interacts vociferously. There are interjections, interruptions, justifications. Priestley, however, varies the pace at critical moments in the play by including long monologues which also draw the main characters into relief. Birling has his two long pompous speeches in Act 1. Sheila and Gerald both have long narrative passages (in Acts 1 and 2 respectively) in which they flesh out the plot. As far as the Inspector is concerned, it is his weighty manner, and the way in which he totally ignores social hierarchy and etiquette, that distinguish him from the other characters. His dramatic final speech stands out as a statement of biblical solemnity: 'We are responsible for each other. And I tell you that the time will soon come when, if men will not learn that lesson, then they will be taught it in fire and blood and anguish.' To some extent Priestley uses language to reflect social position too, although this often involves what the characters say rather than how they say it: we are told, for example, that Mr Birling is rather provincial in his speech, which seems to mean provincial both in accent and in what he says (congratulating cook on the dinner, constantly mentioning his knighthood), and nearly all Mrs Birling's comments are to do with social class. On the other hand, Sheila and Eric, the young people, use occasional slang expressions like 'squiffy' and 'chump', which shock their parents and point up the generation gap.

Dramatic irony

The definition of dramatic irony given in *A Dictionary of Literary Terms* (Longman, York Press) is as follows: 'A feature in many plays; it occurs when the development of the plot allows the audience to possess more information about what is happening than some of the characters themselves have.'

We have already drawn attention to the ironic way in which Priestley undercuts Mr Birling's self-satisfaction by letting him express false optimism about the future. We know, as Mr Birling does not, that the *Titanic* will sink, war will be declared. We also usually know before the characters do what it is the Inspector is going to make them confess to, so we have the ironic pleasure of watching them make their excuses and evasions. To give a specific example: towards the end of Act 2 it is clear to Sheila and the audience that the symmetry of the plot demands that Mrs Birling be the next person to have to admit an involvement with Daisy Renton. So our interest is not in the involvement as such, but in the way in which she will be made to reveal what she knows. In the process the additional horror of the girl's pregnancy is revealed. Again we, the audience (and Sheila), quickly work out that Eric, who is the only person yet to have his involvement with Daisy revealed, must be responsible. The dramatic irony comes from the fact that again Mrs Birling does not work this out for herself. We see her under scrutiny, but still misunderstanding and eventually condemning her own son unknowingly: 'He should be made an example of.'

Another example of this ironic tension is the double ending. The play could have ended with the Inspector's departure, but by allowing three of his characters (Mr and Mrs Birling and Gerald) to wriggle out of the truth and once more condemn themselves out of their own mouths as selfish and hypocritical, Priestley makes his point more forcibly. The ending, though, comes not entirely as a surprise. The air of melodramatic inevitability which surrounds the Inspector's departure actually makes it likely that something will happen. There is also a double irony in the fact that we are still just as hypocritical as the characters on stage. The Inspector has been talking to us too and in so far as we have not changed we are not in a position to judge the characters in the play who do not change either.

Time and *An Inspector Calls*

At the end of the play the audience is left to rewrite the scenario again as they set off home. Will this second version permit the characters to act differently?

The idea of circularity, of making the end another beginning, always fascinated J. B. Priestley and can be seen in a simple form in his first play, *Dangerous Corner* (1932). In the introduction to that play he talks of the device of 'splitting time into two – showing what might have happened . . .', and indeed there are many similarities here with *An Inspector Calls*. In *Dangerous Corner* a 'snug little group' of family and friends is settling down self-contentedly for the evening. They gradually find themselves uncovering the dangerous 'truth' about one of their number, who died in mysterious circumstances. It turns out that they have all been involved in some way or other. By the last act we suspect that nothing will ever be the same again; all the relationships will have to be rewritten. Until the very last scene that is, when the play begins again and this time sleeping dogs are allowed to lie and the opportunity for unpleasant revelations is not taken up. There is no outside agency to parallel the Inspector, and the emphasis is on being honest, rather than responsible; at the same time the audience is made aware of the multiplicity of future possibilities arising out of the present in a way that looks forward to the double ending of *An Inspector Calls*.

In 1937 two plays by Priestley were staged, both of them inspired by his enthusiasm for the time theories of Ouspensky and Dunne. *Time and the Conways* in part develops Dunne's complicated ideas about time. Principally, however, it uses time as a dramatic trick, viewing it, not chronologically, but from a series of vantage points, moving from the present to the future and then back to the present again. Set in 1919, the first act shows us the Conway family celebrating a birthday. Their view of the future is optimistic and positive. Act 2 is set in the 'future' of 1937. The hoped-for potential has not been fulfilled by any of the Conway children. Kay is particularly depressed by this awareness, but her brother Alan tries to comfort her with Dunne-inspired philosophy: 'What we really are is the whole stretch of ourselves, all our time, and when we come to the end of this life, all those selves, all our time, will be us – the real you, the real me. And then perhaps we'll find ourselves in another time, which is only another kind of dream' (*Collected Plays*, volume 1, page 177). Act 3 takes us back to 1919 and the continuation of the birthday party. We now know more about the Conways than they know themselves, although Kay seems to have premonitions about the future, and our knowledge of what will one day happen undercuts the brightness and the gaiety which we know to be transitory. In this play too the possibility of a double ending is hinted at when Mrs Conway wants to tell fortunes, but Kay who has this sense of foreboding about the future that the others lack, prevents her from doing so.

I Have Been Here Before was produced later in 1937, although it had been written – and, unusually for Priestley, rewritten several times – before. It is not nearly so successful a play as *Time and the Conways* because Priestley has not really found a way of assimilating what he wants to say about time convincingly into the plot. On this occasion it is Ouspensky's ideas on time which are behind the play: time moves in spirals, and we relive the same life over and over again; to some of us is accorded the chance to intervene in the cycle. In many ways this is a version of man's struggle to resist his fate by the imposition of his free will.

In Act 1 four characters converge on a Yorkshire inn for the weekend. Görtler, mysteriously foreign in more senses than one, is glad to find Mr and Mrs Ormund and the young schoolmaster Farrant staying there. The three of them all experience an uneasy feeling of déjà-vu, a feeling that they have already lived through this experience with these same people. By the end of Act 2 Farrant and Mrs Ormund are rather miserably, almost inevitably, in love, and we are aware of the chain of dependence that links all the characters together. In Act 3 the time theory is spelt out by Görtler in rather indigestible monologues; he has had a dream about the future, in which Ormund commits suicide and Mrs Ormund and Farrant live together in unhappy penury. He has tried to insert himself into the right year in order to intervene in their lives before this tragedy occurs. He manages to persuade Ormund to accept his wife's departure calmly and almost happily, so this time round there will be no suicide. 'You can return to the old dark circle of existence, dying

endless deaths, or you can break the spell and swing out into new life'
(*Collected Plays*, volume 1, page 264).

To some extent these are the themes of *An Inspector Calls*. The
time angle gives a strongly redemptive tone to all these three
plays – people are offered the chance to improve themselves and
therefore change things for the better, as long as they have the moral
courage to examine the past with ruthless integrity. The time element
becomes a way of stressing the importance of caring for others and of
developing a sense of moral and social responsibility, and at the same
time a mystical, other-worldly, dreamlike atmosphere is created
which seems to imbue the actions of the characters with a greater
significance than they might otherwise have had. The Inspector's role
parallels that of Dr Görtler, but is more lightly and therefore more
successfully managed. They are both outsiders who want to intervene
in the characters' lives because they seem to know what is best for
them. The idea of eternal recurrence which is spelt out in *I Have Been
Here Before* fails to be logically convincing, because, once you
introduce changes into a situation, it is impossible for things to
happen the same way again. In *An Inspector Calls* what is to re-occur
is left to the audience to decide. We are left to imagine that next time
round three of the characters will behave in precisely the same way
again, but that Sheila and Eric may have learnt enough to change
their actions for the better.

In *An Inspector Calls* the tension between two temporal perspec-
tives is also achieved straightforwardly: the play was written in 1944
but is set in 1912, so the time gap includes both world wars (the time
gap in *Time and the Conways* only includes the inter-war years, but in
both cases it allows Priestley to develop his obsession with the
unrealised dreams of both pre-war generations). References are
made by the characters to hopes for a peaceful and prosperous future
that the audience knows will not occur. The need for a sense of social
commitment and for individuals to come to grips with their personal
short-comings is thus emphasised.

J. B. Priestley went through the traumatic experience of trench
warfare in France during World War I, and then had to face the
tragedy of another world war (during which he involved himself in
UNESCO work and gave his talks on the BBC). John Braine suggests
that *An Inspector Calls* is the nearest Priestley ever came
to unburdening himself. The undermining of the Birlings' self-
satisfaction, the horror of the girl's death as a symbol for many other
deaths, the attempt to show the responsibility we all share for the
lives of other people, could all be seen in that light. Certainly the idea
that in the wake of World War II mankind has a lesson to learn in
terms of social responsibility, is never far from the surface of the play,

and the possibility of a new beginning allows room for hope in such a context. The split-time device and the possibility of beginning again serve to underline Priestley's social commitment.

In a more technical sense, Priestley makes sure that the last two years of the dead girl's life are accurately reconstructed. This involves repeated references to months and years from 1910 to 1912, thereby also reinforcing the date of the play's setting in the audience's mind.

The political message of *An Inspector Calls*

Certainly the play contains a deeply felt social message: expressed in fundamentally realistic tones it is emphasised by an atmosphere of mystery and symbolism. Priestley himself talks of the 'heightened reality we know to be unreal', and this is perhaps where we see the influence of Chekhov. The play starts in a carefully reconstructed period dining-room, and the references in the first part of Act 1 remind us constantly of the year we are supposed to be in. Gradually the emphasis shifts away from realistic details; the play begins to deal with universal issues. The language becomes less realistic, the moral message more insistent, yet the audience accepts it as possible because the change has been gradual and gentle. Priestley's account of the badly paid factory workers' attempts to keep body and soul together reminds us of *English Journey* (1934), with its stress on the shared humanity of all classes. Sheila is the character who is most ready to experience this kind of compassion; the Inspector (who is dismissed as a socialist and a crank by Birling) attempts to develop this feeling into one of community, of shared guilt and responsibility. The gradual revelation of each character's involvement with Eva Smith/Daisy Renton stresses this theme.

The Inspector, initially plausible if strange, gradually becomes the mysterious voice of conscience. When he tells the Birling family that men will learn of their responsibility for each other 'in fire and blood and anguish', the biblical hyperbole seems totally acceptable in an Edwardian suburban house. Even if the audience is ready to share the questioning unease with which the Birlings examine the Inspector's behaviour once he has left, it will nevertheless retain a sense of the moral outrage that the Inspector's enquiries have given rise to.

As in an Ibsen play the prosperity and apparent respectability of a middle-class family are shown to be a sham. The message for the audience is that they must question not only the complacency of the Birlings' generation, but also their own. It is in this way that Priestley's commitment to socialism with a small 's' motivates the plot. The political message, as so often with Priestley, is a very general one. Individuals are criticised; the play declares that we all have a responsibility towards one another; but social criticism never becomes more clearly defined than that.

Class and social status

Priestley chooses to make his criticism of his own society through an attack on a comfortably-off middle-class Edwardian family. This is familiar ground for the author, and he has no difficulty in recreating their world, their values, their conversation and even the exact furnishings of their dining-room, as the page-long stage directions indicate. Their social conventions point up their wealth and outlook: it is a world where you dress for dinner, have maids, where the ladies withdraw and leave the men to the port and the serious conversation. This obvious prosperity is implicitly contrasted with Eva Smith's/ Daisy Renton's declining fortunes; she is a conscientious worker with a much stronger sense of moral rectitude than Eric or his parents and yet she is condemned to unemployment, poverty and exploitation. None of the representatives of the comfortably-off middle classes will help her, and she is eventually driven to suicide.

Middle-class solidarity is accompanied here by hypocrisy and snobbery. Gerald Croft is detached from all this by the security of his position at the top of the social ladder, but Mr and Mrs Birling are guilty of too many of what Sheila calls 'these silly pretences'. They are falsely protective of their daughter, unable to imagine that she can have had any contact with the seamy side of life. They cannot believe that an alderman could go looking for a prostitute, any more than that their son could drink too much, let alone get a girl pregnant. They are depressingly, unquestioningly sure of their values. They are also dominated by a determination both to safeguard their 'respectability' and improve their social position. Mr Birling is not a landowner, but a new arrival into the middle classes thanks to his wealth which has been gained through trade. Gerald has a mother who comes from the landed aristocracy, a father who is a knight, so to Sheila's family her engagement represents welcome social recognition. Mrs Birling, who is her husband's social superior, is forced through snobbishness into being unnaturally controlled and confident, while he desperately tries to protect his chances of getting a knighthood, and makes a fool of himself when he attempts to use his social superiority to undermine the Inspector's authority. Sheila and Eric are the unthinking inheritors of their parents' way of life who readily assume the privileges of wealth, until the Inspector arrives to remind them of the existence of people like Eva Smith, equally deserving if not equally rich.

Changing values

At the end of the play Sheila and Eric are the only two characters committed to change. They reflect the hope of the younger generation of 1912 (and by implication of 1945) to build a new world.

The world represented in the play is a changing one. Mr Birling is a 'nouveau riche', a 'hard-headed business man' who has been made rich by the growth of industry in a Midland town. Eva Smith's life too was touched by this growth of industry. She was country-bred but had come to seek work in the city's factories. Yet in fact Britain's industrial power is about to be overtaken. The change which we know is soon to come about, will come through two world wars.

There is a change too in the possibilities of social mobility. The respectable poor like Eva Smith/Daisy Renton had always easily slipped down to the bottom of the social ladder. But now upward mobility can be fast too. Not only can Mr Birling become rich, but he can send his son to public school and university, marry his daughter into the landed aristocracy, and even hope to gain a knighthood.

These ambitions are not without a price; the Birling family unity is threatened. The bonds of affection that the family claims to possess are shown to be worthless. By the end of the play Sheila and Eric are ashamed of their parents. Eric has always distrusted them, and gone his own wild way rather than confide in them. Mr Birling tries to assert his authority, but it is based on his pomposity alone, and his children are impatient with it. Mr and Mrs Birling are kept together by a sense of purpose, but it does not lead them to sympathise with, or console or try to understand their children. The generation gap has manifested itself, and Eric and Sheila are able to show how different they are.

The family disagreements draw attention to the different outlooks of the two generations, and also to the final message of the play, which is a plea for change, a change in human nature first, then a change in society. People must become more supportive of each other. They must also develop a different concept of social duty from the one that protects the Birling parents from self-criticism. Mrs Birling can tell herself that she is not to blame for Daisy's death, that she did her duty. Mr Birling thinks he is a respectable citizen, because unlike his children he can make a distinction between a private and a public scandal. What the Inspector wants to change is exactly this. They all have to learn that private behaviour has public consequences.

Characters

Since the majority of Priestley's plays are set in the homes of middle-class families his repertoire of characters is bound to consist of variations of the same types: bright young things, serious spinsters, fathers too absorbed in their work to understand what is happening to others, and so on. Many of his plots too involve an outside catalyst which disturbs the stability of these same middle-class homes.

Inspector Goole

Inevitably it is the character of the Inspector which has the greatest impact. The symbolism of his role and the plot are closely entwined. He arrives just after Mr Birling has been enunciating his personal philosophy of life: every man for himself. The Inspector sets out to prove to the assembled company the dangers of such a philosophy. From his entrance he is at odds with the party mood. Unlike the Birlings and Gerald, who are in evening dress, he is dressed in a plain suit. The stage directions tell us that he 'creates at once an impression of massiveness, solidity and purposefulness'. This forceful presence allows him to control the five other characters: not only does he induce them to admit their involvement with Eva Smith or Daisy Renton, but he controls their behaviour on stage, saying who can and who cannot leave, or who can see the photograph, or whose turn it is to 'confess' next. He will admit no side-stepping, no excuses. While he is on stage the characters cannot avoid being stripped bare of their dishonesties: 'somehow he makes you', says Sheila (Act 2).

He has in his possession Eva Smith's diary, and from the events recorded in it he builds up a picture of her character too. He wants the Birlings and Gerald to admit that their lives and their characters were involved in hers. By constantly reminding them of her horrible death he wants them to feel responsible for their actions which, taken one by one, might not have had such dreadful consequences. His aim is to force them to see this truth, to reach this understanding. Clearly then his role is that of an all-knowing outsider (remember Dr Görtler in *I Have Been Here Before*).

The message of the play, however, dictates that the Inspector can only be an agent: he can try to compel the Birlings and Gerald to change their view of the world, but in the end it is up to each individual to understand himself or herself. To this extent the Inspector is less real than the other five. First and foremost he has to be a manipulator: of consciences, but also of the plot. He is super-human and unreal. Even his name, Goole, has mysterious and ghostly connotations.

Nevertheless, like the characters in the play, we, the audience, are taken in by him. Although it is clear from early on that he is not in the Birlings' house for a simple police enquiry, he does have some of the attributes of a typical police inspector, even if these are somewhat intensified: his singleness of purpose, his control of the way in which he wants to 'inspect' the characters in particular. At the end of Act 3, when with Gerald's help the Birlings try to prove to themselves that he was not really an inspector, it is his rudeness to Mr and Mrs Birling that they remember as being atypical. It is indeed this failure to observe social conventions which isolates him from the elegant celebration he has just interrupted. Priestley's skill lies in the way that he allows the Inspector to grow steadily more distinct, and more messianic as the play develops.

Sheila Birling

She is described in the stage directions as a 'pretty girl in her early twenties, very pleased with life and rather excited'. At the beginning of the play she is unthinkingly selfish, but she is ready to learn: she is sensitive and easily moved, and she is also observant and intelligent.

In Act 1, almost without the Inspector's help, she begins to see the world through his eyes: she realises that Gerald's absence the previous summer is somehow important. The minute the Inspector tells her of the suicide she identifies sympathetically with the girl: 'I've been so happy tonight . . . What was she like? Quite young?' (Act 1). Even before she learns of her own involvement in the death she is trying to overcome a lack of understanding: she sees the girl as a person rather than as cheap labour as her father does. She is genuinely remorseful when she learns how her whim caused the girl's dismissal; simultaneously she is upset that she will never be able to return to the shop. So she is still at this stage two people: one who is very bound up in her own social class, her wedding, and so on; the other who is emotionally sensitive and open to change.

In Act 2 she develops further: she copes with Gerald's confession; she is the first to understand the Inspector's real role; she sees the trap her mother will fall into over her accusations about the father of the unborn child. In Act 3, like Eric, she desperately wants to have learnt something, to have changed.

She stands out as the person who has gone beyond social hypocrisy and has understood the Inspector's message: she will feel responsible for other people in the future. Her character is prefigured in several of Priestley's earlier plays: Olwen in *Dangerous Corner* and Kay in *Time and the Conways* are both young women who are sensitive enough to appreciate that beyond the family gathering in which they find themselves involved there is a world where honesty and truth are all-important.

Eric Birling

Eric is 'not quite at ease, half shy, half assertive'. He is young and rather silly.

In one sense his guilt and involvement in the girl's death are worse than anybody else's. Like Sheila he is guilty of thoughtlessness, but in his case the consequences are far more serious. He has been irresponsible all through: he drinks, he steals, he gets the girl pregnant. Nevertheless Priestley places him with the young ones who can learn and who can change. He does admit everything freely, and, like Sheila, wishes that his parents too could change. Some of the blame for his behaviour lies with his parents. From the beginning of the play there is friction between them and Eric, and it becomes clear that his parents were the last people he thought of when he needed money and help: 'you're not the kind of father a chap could go to when he's in trouble' (Act 3). He behaves unthinkingly, even answering his parents back quite rudely, but he does not seek to evade responsibility for his part in the girl's death.

Mr Birling

He is 'heavy-looking . . . in his middle-fifties . . . provincial in his speech'. He does not change over the course of the play, any more than his wife does. Of all the characters he is the one most pleased with himself. The engagement between Sheila and Gerald matters greatly to him because it forges useful business links for him. When he makes his speech to Eric and Gerald this self-satisfaction really comes out. Within the logic of the play he has to be the one to make the hard-headed comment that 'a man has to mind his own business and look after himself' (Act 1).

He blusters his way through the play; he tries to use his social superiority to undermine the Inspector's authority; he uses the fact that he is their father to subdue Eric and Sheila; he is most concerned about the effect of a public scandal on his chances of being knighted. He is totally unable to understand the Inspector's message about responsibility for others. We all sense that he would sack the girl a second time. He is unaware of his double standards when he wants Sheila to be protected from the nastiness of the girl's story. When the Inspector leaves, Birling's one desire is to revert to the normality he understands. He has no sympathy for Sheila's or Eric's view of events but is at a loss for the right action to take until Gerald takes charge.

Priestley is skilful enough not to make Birling totally dislikeable. His naïve belief that he can control the Inspector, and even his self-centredness are almost pitiable because he is never entirely in control of events.

Mrs Birling

Mrs Birling on the other hand has no redeeming features. She is 'a rather cold woman and her husband's social superior'. Priestley makes this coldness her most unsympathetic trait. Clearly she is more intelligent than Birling, but her lack of imagination and conscience makes her brand of self-righteousness peculiarly unlikeable. She has no idea of how other people live, and no desire to know. This enables her to be almost totally unmoved by the Inspector and by what he reveals to her. It becomes clear that the fact that she refused to give her money was the precipitating cause of the girl's suicide, and thereby of the death of her own unborn grandchild. Nevertheless after the Inspector's departure she quickly recovers herself and is soon thanking Gerald for his clever handling of affairs.

Gerald Croft

Priestley uses the character of Gerald Croft to throw light both on the Birling parents who are too set in their social ways to be changed by the Inspector's visit, and on the Birling children who are certainly very responsive to the Inspector's message, but possibly in a slightly naïve and hysterical way.

Gerald is in his thirties, so he is between the two generations of Birlings in age. He is 'very much the easy well-bred young man-about-town'. His mother is Lady Croft, his father owns a rival and more successful business than Birling's, so, unlike Birling, he is not trying to climb out of the middle class. His social ease is apparent at the beginning of the play when he handles Mr Birling's confidential hints about an imminent knighthood very tactfully. At the end of the play he is able to distance himself enough from events to find a socially acceptable explanation for what has happened to them all.

According to the Inspector he comes out of the involvement with Daisy Renton best because 'he made her happy for a time' (Act 3). Certainly he has the quality of straightforwardness which enables him to come through the evening. Sheila, who is wiser now, has learnt to respect him for his honesty; Mrs Birling congratulates him for unmasking the Inspector.

Edna

The maid's presence is only a token one. Her most important function is to announce the Inspector's arrival.

Eva Smith/Daisy Renton

She never appears on the stage, we do not know her real name and we never see her photograph. Yet the last two years of her life are central to the plot, and Priestley uses both the quality of her life and her personality as a foil to the four Birlings and their guest.Her particularly ugly death contrasts with the elegant dining-room atmosphere. Her conscientiousness, her scruples, her consideration for others make her a very different person from those the Inspector criticises for their lack of responsibility. Even though by the end of the play we have a clear idea of her movements during the last two years of her life, she remains a shadowy character. We know that she had dark eyes, and was pretty enough for Sheila to be jealous of her and for Gerald and Eric to be attracted to her. In many ways she is a counterpoint to the Inspector. Like him she remains a symbolic figure, and one who carries the weight of the plot. Her squalid fate, despite her noble qualities, acts as a plea for compassion and understanding in the rest of us. In his final speech the Inspector reminds us of this: 'But just remember this. One Eva Smith has gone – but there are millions and millions and millions of Eva Smiths and John Smiths still left with us, with their lives, their hopes and fears, their suffering and chance of happiness, all intertwined with our lives, with what we think and say and do' (Act 3).

Part 4

Hints for study

Using Parts 2 and 3

The main themes and incidents of *An Inspector Calls* are all interrelated. A consideration of the *plot*, and particularly of the ending of the play, takes us to Priestley's ideas on *time*. They in turn draw our attention to his dissatisfaction with the post-war world and the resulting *social criticism*. One of the ways in which he criticises the society of 1945 is to show the older generation entrenched in their selfish world, but the younger generation more open to appeals to their humanity. So we move on to *characterisation*.

A good way of studying these ideas more closely is by using the information from Parts 2 and 3 of this book:

The summaries in Part 2 are your obvious guide to the *plot*. It is very tightly constructed: the Inspector forces first Mr Birling and Sheila (in Act 1), then Gerald and Mrs Birling (in Act 2) and finally Eric (in Act 3) to see how they share responsibility for the girl's death. When discussing the plot never forget how the ending allows for the play to begin again, so that you can never say that anything is definitely resolved. If you are interested in the more technical aspects of Priestley's craft as a playwright the first four sections in Part 3 ('Reading a play', 'Technical considerations', 'Genre' and 'Language') will suggest to you what details to look for in order to understand how Priestley dramatises the plot.

This brings us to the section on 'Time and *An Inspector Calls*'. The idea of making the ending another beginning is discussed in detail there. The fact that the play was first performed in 1945 but set in 1912 is also emphasised.

This perspective on a world before World War I is used to highlight Mr Birling's almost ridiculous self-satisfaction, which is where Priestley begins his social criticism. The author's first attacks are directed against the prejudices which result from the family's social status. These are discussed in the section on 'Class and social status'. Priestley quickly moves towards a more general criticism of the Birling family as lacking in compassion. You will find a discussion of this theme in the section on 'The political message of *An Inspector Calls*'.

The most obvious approach to the play and to its major themes is, however, through the characters. The Inspector is in a sense the least interesting, as in the end his main role is to act as a mysterious outside agent forcing the truth out of the five 'real' characters. Mr and Mrs Birling can be considered together: they belong to the same generation and to a large extent share the same attitudes to life. Sheila and Eric can be similarly paired off: they are both in their twenties and are receptive to the Inspector's message. Gerald Croft is perhaps the most interesting character, as he manages to gain everyone's respect as the night develops. A close look at the section on 'Characters' will help you think about these issues more deeply.

Selecting suitable quotations

Priestley's style is straightforward and his handling of dialogue is realistic: people answer one another and interact with one another in such a way that on the whole it is difficult to isolate short memorable utterances from their context. The exceptions are Mr Birling's two attempts at speech-making in Act 1 and the Inspector's parting words. For this reason the sentence from Mr Birling's speech – 'a man has to mind his own business and look after himself and his own' (Act 1) – and the sentences from the Inspector's speech – 'We don't live alone. We are members of one body. We are responsible for each other' (Act 3) – are worth learning by heart. They neatly encapsulate the plot, from Mr Birling's self-satisfaction at the beginning of the play to the lesson the Inspector hopes he has taught the family by the end of the play.

Of course, the fact that it is not particularly appropriate to memorise many quotations does not mean that you cannot refer to the play in detail. In answering questions on any of the major themes or characterisations you will have to. The best method is to understand and remember the movement of the plot extremely well. This includes remembering where and why each act begins and ends, who is and who is not present on the stage during a scene, and so on. Then you are in a position to paraphrase in your own words what one character says to another. For instance, you can refer in detail to Mr Birling's intial rudeness to the Inspector like this: when the Inspector first arrives Mr Birling tries hard to impress him by his social superiority. First he reminds the Inspector that he was an alderman, and is still a judge. Then he points out that he plays golf with the Chief Constable. None of this impresses the Inspector at all.

On the other hand, you should be able to identify and comment on any quotations from the play that you are given. Study the following passage and try and comment on it with reference to the characters, scenes or plot of the play:

Oh well – put like that, there's something in what you say. Still, I can't accept any responsibility. If we were all responsible for everything that happened to everybody we'd had anything to do with, it would be very awkward, wouldn't it?

Selected questions

(1) What is the effect of the telephone call at the end of the play?
(2) What impression do we have of the Birlings before the arrival of the Inspector?
(3) What changes occur in the relationship between Sheila and Gerald during the course of the play?
(4) *An Inspector Calls* has been described as a play of social criticism. What is being criticised?
(5) Which of the characters has changed most by the end of the play?
(6) Describe the way in which the Birling family begin to believe that the Inspector is not a genuine policeman.
(7) Consider the diagram and furniture and property list for Act 1 of *An Inspector Calls* below and say how they help set the scene and the mood of the play.

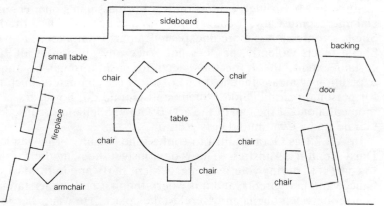

On stage: Dining table. On it: Silver candlesticks, flower arrangement (centre piece), dish of fruit and nuts, nut-crackers, matches in stand, box of cigarettes, 5 dessert plates, knives, forks and spoons, 5 port glasses, 5 napkins

Sideboard. On it: 1 silver candlestick, champagne cooler, empty champagne bottle, 5 champagne glasses, silver tray with 5 tumblers, water jug, port decanter, soda syphon

Desk. On it: Ashtray, table lamp, pen, inkwell, blotter, cigars

6 dining-room chairs

Armchair

Fire-irons

On mantelpiece: Marble clock, 2 bronze figures

On small table near fireplace: Telephone directory

Specimen answers

(3) What changes occur in the relationship between Sheila and Gerald during the course of the play?

The play begins with a dinner party to celebrate Sheila's engagement to Gerald Croft. It is a quiet family affair, but through the Edwardian conventions and restraints we see that the couple's relationship is both gently teasing and quietly tender. There is a toast; Gerald presents Sheila with a ring: everything is as it should be. Sheila is a normal, happy young girl, unaware of the privileges her social position gives her. Gerald is a more mature man, who is looked up to by his prospective father-in-law, not just for his social standing, but also for his level-headedness.

Into this contented family party the Inspector is introduced, with his news of Eva Smith's sordid suicide. Before the act is over Mr Birling has admitted having sacked her and Sheila has told how she persuaded the shop she patronises to dismiss the girl. Gerald is present during all this, although he makes moves to leave. His attitude to Mr Birling's confession is a businessman's one: commercial interest must always come before human interest. His attitude to Sheila's confession is more unexpected: apart from a look, to which Sheila reacts violently, he does not voice any opinion at all. To a certain extent, the Inspector's need to push through his inquiry expeditiously means that he does not allow the characters much time for personal recriminations. Sheila and Gerald do, however, have a moment alone at the end of the act. By now, Sheila has realised that Gerald knew Eva Smith/Daisy Renton.

In Act 2 it is Gerald's turn to confess: he is guilty of having made Daisy Renton his mistress. This is obviously a shocking thing to have to confess to during your own engagement party and in front of your fiancée and her parents, and it is where the first real, understandable quarrel between Sheila and Gerald takes place. He wants her to go; she needs to share her burden of guilt and insists on staying. It is to Gerald's credit that he carries off his eventual confession, and although Sheila starts by making heavily ironic remarks about his behaviour, she is won over by his honest and straightforward attitude. Inevitably she hands him his ring back, but she admits that she now respects him more than she did before, and we, the audience, accept this. Throughout the play Sheila grows in moral stature. She learns to view the world from a new perspective, which is a less selfish one. Gerald proves himself by his honesty and straight-

forwardness. To this extent, Priestley uses the lack of any great interaction between the engaged couple to advantage. They are both
above such petty-minded quarrels. Gerald's confession is indeed
central to the recasting of their relationship. As Sheila says: 'You and
I aren't the same people who sat down to dinner here. We'd have to
start all over again, getting to know each other – ' (Act 2). It is the
start of a deeper, more real relationship. Sheila already suspected
that Gerald had not been honest with her, but convention had
required her to accept his excuses. Now she is free to reject such
hypocrisy. This change of heart is managed very economically by
Priestley.

In Act 3, however, their relationship does not develop smoothly.
Gerald has briefly left the house in order to calm down, but also, it
transpires on his return, to ascertain whether or not the Inspector was
genuine. We see that for him the most important thing is to gloss over
moral upsets. Originally he just kept his summer affair with Daisy
Renton from Sheila, but now that deceit is not enough he has to find
another way to prevent it spoiling the surface of his life. Sheila has
moved in the opposite direction and is desperate to see everyone
committed to an unselfish, moral view. Again there is little dramatic
interaction between the couple, but when Sheila refuses the ring
again it comes as no surprise.

According to the Inspector, Gerald acquitted himself better than
the others, yet in Act 3 his character does not really stand up to close
examination. He will risk hypocrisy and deceit to avoid trouble. We
can only imagine what the clearly more sensitive Sheila feels. She
says she respects him more, but we are left wondering how to
evaluate his infidelity. The fact that Sheila can cope with it shows that
the change in their relationship comes through her. She has the sen-
sitivity to see that nothing will be the same again, but she is not
tempted to an unconditional vilification of Gerald. In many ways he
is the dependable man she said she would marry. But nothing is the
same at the end of the play, and we can only wonder what will happen
a second time round.

---

(4) *An Inspector Calls* has been described as a play of social criticism.
What is being criticised?

The criticisms that J. B. Priestley levels at society operate at two
levels in his play. First there is a particularised attack on what the
Birling family represent, both from the point of view of their unfair
social privileges, and from the point of view of the selfishness that
these engender in terms of their lack of any sense of responsibility for
Eva Smith's/Daisy Renton's death. From this base Priestley is able to

move on to a wider, more generalised criticism of modern society which has brought about two world wars as a result of its refusal to see that men must accept more responsibility for each other. The device of setting the play in 1912, although it was written in 1944, serves to emphasise both levels of social criticism. Birling's ridiculously optimistic speech about progress in Act 1 shows him as a representative of his class failing to understand the way society is evolving. The Inspector's 'fire and blood and anguish' speech in Act 3 summarises what the Birlings themselves are supposed to have learnt from the evening's experience, but also gives a moral message to society at large, as represented by the audience. Priestley offers us, as the Inspector offers the Birlings, the chance to change.

Priestley's criticism of the Birlings takes the form of an attack on the privileges of class. Eva Smith's/Daisy Renton's death is a symbol of their ignorance of how the other half lives. They not only take their own material well-being for granted, but their assumptions are that there should be one rule for the rich and one for the poor. They are guilty of tunnel vision. The prosperous and comfortable dining-room that they never leave is a symbol of their lack of interest in others. Outside there may be a world of shop-girls, factory strikes, unemployment, prostitution; but it does not affect them (or so they think) and therefore they ignore it. They perceive the world as a place in which to make useful connections, by playing golf with the Chief Constable, or by finding a good catch for their daughter to marry. Until the Inspector's arrival they have successfully ignored what they did not want to see: Alderman Meggarty consorting with 'women of the town' in the Palace bar, or Eric's drinking. The Inspector holds a mirror up to the Birlings' life-style. Without his 'inquiry' they had no awareness that they had done wrong. The play attempts to shake their consciences and give them the chance to become more socially aware. They have avoided doing so by operating double standards. Mrs Birling's benevolent society is for 'deserving cases'; Mr Birling on the other hand thinks of his women workers as 'cheap labour'. So Daisy Renton's chance of moving from one category to the other is remote. To begin with Sheila sees nothing wrong in getting a girl dismissed from Milwards; it is acceptable for Gerald and Eric to have affairs on the side; but the object of their attentions is unthinkingly criticised for her role in the same situation.

So on one level the play criticises all five main characters for their selfishness, their moral blindness. The awareness that the Inspector forces upon them, not only of their involvement and responsibility for Eva Smith's/Daisy Renton's suicide, but of the selfishness and hypocrisy that lay behind it, is meant to take effect at an individual level. We want to see which of the five will change, which of them will think and behave more unselfishly in the future. There is, however, a more general message to be abstracted from the play too. This level of interpretation is indicated by the unreal, depersonalised character of the Inspector. If he is not the 'Socialist crank' Mr Birling suspects him of being then he must be the voice of conscience, raising the awareness of the audience as well as the Birlings. Eva Smith's/Daisy Renton's suicide is only an example of what man can do to man. The deeper moral message of the play is one of mutual responsibility, and with this comes the implied criticism of any society that does not follow this principle.

---

(5) Which of the characters has changed most by the end of the play?

In the stage directions at the beginning of Act 1 we are told that the five characters are all 'pleased with themselves'. As the evening develops all five will have their outward self-confidence shaken as a result of the Inspector's visit, but the change will not be a permanent one for all of them.

Even before the Inspector arrives Priestley makes sure that his characters are differentiated. The relaxed family gathering has hidden tensions. Mr Birling is engaged in social climbing; Gerald is politely flattering; Mrs Birling is trying to make sure her husband observes the social niceties. Eric seems enthusiastic but possibly misguided. Sheila seems the most straightforwardly honest. By the time the Inspector leaves each one of them has had to accept his or her involvement in the chain of events that led up to Daisy Renton's suicide: Mr Birling had used his power as an employer to sack her even though she was a good worker; Sheila and Mrs Birling used their social standing to make life impossible for her; Eric by behaving thoughtlessly like a spoilt child helped to bring about her suicide. Gerald, as the Inspector makes clear, was more affectionate, if equally cavalier, in his relationship with her.

Once the Inspector has left, Priestley gives us a closer insight into the characters. In the case of Mr and Mrs Birling and Gerald, social status reasserts itself. They feel more powerful than this 'fraudulent' Inspector; they pour themselves another drink; they are pleased with themselves again. Only Eric and Sheila want the change that the Inspector has brought about in their view of the world to be a permanent one. As the more mature and thoughtful of the two, it is Sheila who convinces the audience that she has changed the most.

Priestley has given her the most sensitive character, and so the potential for a commitment to the idea of shared moral responsibility is in her from the beginning. The minute she hears of the suicide she feels sympathy and horror. She feels instant regret for her own action

which led to the girl being sacked from Milwards. She appreciates
Gerald's honesty and is able to forgive him, although she knows that
their relationship will need to be re-evaluated. She attempts to
persuade her mother to adopt a kinder frame of mind. She is socially
less hypocritical than her parents; she has noticed more about Eric's
drinking, Gerald's absence and Alderman Meggarty's behaviour
than they could allow themselves to. In Act 1 she has to cope with her
own guilt, in Act 2 with Gerald's betrayal of her, yet she learns
tolerance of others through understanding of herself.

Before the Inspector's arrival she was a happy girl on the night of
her engagement. By the end of the play she is almost fighting her
parents to persuade them they have been given a lesson to learn: 'I
tell you – whoever that Inspector was, it was anything but a joke.
You knew it then. You began to learn something. And now you've
stopped' (Act 3). Unlike theirs, Sheila's new view of the world is
permanent. As the Inspector has explained earlier on, 'the young
ones [are] more impressionable', that is to say they are less set in
their social ways.

Sheila's changed view of the world is matched at the other end of
the scale by her mother's determined refusal to accept that she has
done anything wrong. It is this contrast that gives effect to the change
in Sheila. If there are still people in the world who can justify turning
away a pregnant and destitute Daisy Renton in the name of duty,
then we need a commitment on the part of the younger generation to
change this situation. In this way Sheila is made to carry the social
message of the play. Not only has she changed the most, but she has
inherited the Inspector's mantle and must constantly remind the rest
of her family of his message.

Note: when answering questions always remember:
(1) to quote directly from the play, or to paraphrase closely;
(2) to interpret the question at a general level in the first paragraph;
(3) to come back to the question in the last paragraph and sum up
    your argument;
(4) to use your knowledge of the development of the plot in the
    middle paragraphs.

Part 5

Suggestions for further reading

The text

The text of *An Inspector Calls* used in these notes is that published by Heinemann Educational Books, London, 1987, in the Hereford Plays series. This is the latest reprint, with a short, useful introduction.

Other plays by J. B. Priestley

In 1948, 1949 and 1950 Heinemann, London, published three volumes of Priestley's *Collected Plays*. They are a representative collection of his best-known plays, and each volume has an introduction by the author.

Volume I
Dangerous Corner (1932)
Eden End (1934)
Time and the Conways (1937)
I Have Been Here Before (1937)
Johnson over Jordan (1939)
Music at Night (1937)
The Linden Tree (1947)

Volume II
Laburnum Grove (1933)
Bees on the Boat Deck (1936)
When We Are Married (1938)
Goodnight, Children (1942)
The Golden Fleece (1948)
How Are They at Home? (1944)
Ever Since Paradise (1947)

Volume III
Cornelius (1935)
People at Sea (1937)
They Came to a City (1943)
Desert Highway (1944)
An Inspector Calls (1945)
Home is Tomorrow (1948)
Summer Day's Dream (1949)

Autobiographical reminiscences

Much autobiographical detail can be found in the numerous essays and articles Priestley wrote during his long life-time. Listed here are five books he subtitled as autobiography.

Midnight on the Desert (1937)
Rain upon Godshill (1939)
Thoughts in the Wilderness (1957)
Margin Released (1962)
Instead of the Trees (1977)

Criticism

The following are general critical studies, not devoted solely to *An Inspector Calls*.

ATKINS, JOHN: *J. B. Priestley: The Last of the Sages*, John Calder, London, 1981.

BRAINE, JOHN: *J. B. Priestley*, Weidenfeld and Nicolson, London, 1978. An impressionistic and possibly too flattering study.

BROME, VINCENT: *J. B. Priestley*, Hamish Hamilton, London, 1988. The first posthumous biography, a very comprehensive account of his life with surprisingly little on *An Inspector Calls*.

YOUNG, KENNETH: *J. B. Priestley* in the Writers and their Work series, Longman for the British Council, London, 1977. A brief basic survey of Priestley's life and works.

The author of these notes

KATIE GRAY studied French and Italian at the University of Oxford. She has taught these two languages in a variety of different institutions and has been an Open University tutor for ten years. In 1988 she was awarded an MSc in Applied Linguistics at the University of Edinburgh. She is currently Senior Tutor at the Centre for English Language Teaching at Stirling University.

York Notes: list of titles

CHINUA ACHEBE
A Man of the People
Arrow of God
Things Fall Apart

EDWARD ALBEE
Who's Afraid of Virginia Woolf?

ELECHI AMADI
The Concubine

ANONYMOUS
Beowulf
Everyman

AYI KWEI ARMAH
The Beautyful Ones Are Not Yet Born

W. H. AUDEN
Selected Poems

JANE AUSTEN
Emma
Mansfield Park
Northanger Abbey
Persuasion
Pride and Prejudice
Sense and Sensibility

HONORÉ DE BALZAC
Le Père Goriot

SAMUEL BECKETT
Waiting for Godot

SAUL BELLOW
Henderson, The Rain King

ARNOLD BENNETT
Anna of the Five Towns
The Card

WILLIAM BLAKE
Songs of Innocence, Songs of Experience

ROBERT BOLT
A Man For All Seasons

HAROLD BRIGHOUSE
Hobson's Choice

ANNE BRONTË
The Tenant of Wildfell Hall

CHARLOTTE BRONTË
Jane Eyre

EMILY BRONTË
Wuthering Heights

ROBERT BROWNING
Men and Women

JOHN BUCHAN
The Thirty-Nine Steps

JOHN BUNYAN
The Pilgrim's Progress

BYRON
Selected Poems

GEOFFREY CHAUCER
Prologue to the Canterbury Tales
The Clerk's Tale
The Franklin's Tale
The Knight's Tale
The Merchant's Tale
The Miller's Tale
The Nun's Priest's Tale
The Pardoner's Tale
The Wife of Bath's Tale
Troilus and Criseyde

SAMUEL TAYLOR COLERIDGE
Selected Poems

SIR ARTHUR CONAN DOYLE
The Hound of the Baskervilles

WILLIAM CONGREVE
The Way of the World

JOSEPH CONRAD
Heart of Darkness
Nostromo
Victory

STEPHEN CRANE
The Red Badge of Courage

BRUCE DAWE
Selected Poems

WALTER DE LA MARE
Selected Poems

DANIEL DEFOE
A Journal of the Plague Year
Moll Flanders
Robinson Crusoe

CHARLES DICKENS
A Tale of Two Cities
Bleak House
David Copperfield
Dombey and Son
Great Expectations
Hard Times
Little Dorrit
Oliver Twist
The Pickwick Papers

EMILY DICKINSON
Selected Poems

JOHN DONNE
Selected Poems

JOHN DRYDEN
Selected Poems

GERALD DURRELL
My Family and Other Animals

GEORGE ELIOT
Middlemarch
Silas Marner
The Mill on the Floss

T. S. ELIOT
Four Quartets
Murder in the Cathedral
Selected Poems
The Cocktail Party
The Waste Land

J. G. FARRELL
The Siege of Krishnapur

WILLIAM FAULKNER
Absalom, Absalom!
The Sound and the Fury

HENRY FIELDING
Joseph Andrews
Tom Jones

F. SCOTT FITZGERALD
Tender is the Night
The Great Gatsby

GUSTAVE FLAUBERT
Madame Bovary

E. M. FORSTER
A Passage to India
Howards End

JOHN FOWLES
The French Lieutenant's Woman

ATHOL FUGARD
Selected Plays

JOHN GALSWORTHY
Strife

MRS GASKELL
North and South
WILLIAM GOLDING
Lord of the Flies
The Spire
OLIVER GOLDSMITH
She Stoops to Conquer
The Vicar of Wakefield
ROBERT GRAVES
Goodbye to All That
GRAHAM GREENE
Brighton Rock
The Heart of the Matter
The Power and the Glory
WILLIS HALL
The Long and the Short and the Tall
THOMAS HARDY
Far from the Madding Crowd
Jude the Obscure
Selected Poems
Tess of the D'Urbervilles
The Mayor of Casterbridge
The Return of the Native
The Trumpet Major
The Woodlanders
Under the Greenwood Tree
L. P. HARTLEY
The Go-Between
The Shrimp and the Anemone
NATHANIEL HAWTHORNE
The Scarlet Letter
SEAMUS HEANEY
Selected Poems
JOSEPH HELLER
Catch-22
ERNEST HEMINGWAY
A Farewell to Arms
For Whom the Bell Tolls
The Old Man and the Sea
HERMANN HESSE
Steppenwolf
BARRY HINES
Kes
HOMER
The Iliad
The Odyssey
ANTHONY HOPE
The Prisoner of Zenda
GERARD MANLEY HOPKINS
Selected Poems
RICHARD HUGHES
A High Wind in Jamaica
TED HUGHES
Selected Poems
THOMAS HUGHES
Tom Brown's Schooldays
ALDOUS HUXLEY
Brave New World
HENRIK IBSEN
A Doll's House
Ghosts
HENRY JAMES
The Ambassadors
The Portrait of a Lady
Washington Square
SAMUEL JOHNSON
Rasselas
BEN JONSON
The Alchemist
Volpone
JAMES JOYCE
A Portrait of the Artist as a Young Man
Dubliners

JOHN KEATS
Selected Poems
PHILIP LARKIN
Selected Poems
D. H. LAWRENCE
Selected Short Stories
Sons and Lovers
The Rainbow
Women in Love
CAMARA LAYE
L'Enfant Noir
HARPER LEE
To Kill a Mocking-Bird
LAURIE LEE
Cider with Rosie
THOMAS MANN
Tonio Kröger
CHRISTOPHER MARLOWE
Doctor Faustus
ANDREW MARVELL
Selected Poems
W. SOMERSET MAUGHAM
Selected Short Stories
GAVIN MAXWELL
Ring of Bright Water
J. MEADE FALKNER
Moonfleet
HERMAN MELVILLE
Moby Dick
THOMAS MIDDLETON
Women Beware Women
THOMAS MIDDLETON and WILLIAM ROWLEY
The Changeling
ARTHUR MILLER
A View from the Bridge
Death of a Salesman
The Crucible
JOHN MILTON
Paradise Lost I & II
Paradise Lost IV & IX
Selected Poems
V. S. NAIPAUL
A House for Mr Biswas
ROBERT O'BRIEN
Z for Zachariah
SEAN O'CASEY
Juno and the Paycock
GABRIEL OKARA
The Voice
EUGENE O'NEILL
Mourning Becomes Electra
GEORGE ORWELL
Animal Farm
Nineteen Eighty-four
JOHN OSBORNE
Look Back in Anger
WILFRED OWEN
Selected Poems
ALAN PATON
Cry, The Beloved Country
THOMAS LOVE PEACOCK
Nightmare Abbey and Crotchet Castle
HAROLD PINTER
The Caretaker
SYLVIA PLATH
Selected Works
PLATO
The Republic
ALEXANDER POPE
Selected Poems

J. B. PRIESTLEY
An Inspector Calls
THOMAS PYNCHON
The Crying of Lot 49
SIR WALTER SCOTT
Ivanhoe
Quentin Durward
The Heart of Midlothian
Waverley
PETER SHAFFER
The Royal Hunt of the Sun
WILLIAM SHAKESPEARE
A Midsummer Night's Dream
Antony and Cleopatra
As You Like It
Coriolanus
Cymbeline
Hamlet
Henry IV Part I
Henry IV Part II
Henry V
Julius Caesar
King Lear
Love's Labour's Lost
Macbeth
Measure for Measure
Much Ado About Nothing
Othello
Richard II
Richard III
Romeo and Juliet
Sonnets
The Merchant of Venice
The Taming of the Shrew
The Tempest
The Winter's Tale
Troilus and Cressida
Twelfth Night
GEORGE BERNARD SHAW
Androcles and the Lion
Arms and the Man
Caesar and Cleopatra
Candida
Major Barbara
Pygmalion
Saint Joan
The Devil's Disciple
MARY SHELLEY
Frankenstein
PERCY BYSSHE SHELLEY
Selected Poems
RICHARD BRINSLEY SHERIDAN
The School for Scandal
The Rivals
R. C. SHERRIFF
Journey's End
WOLE SOYINKA
The Road
EDMUND SPENSER
The Faerie Queene (Book I)
JOHN STEINBECK
Of Mice and Men
The Grapes of Wrath
The Pearl

LAURENCE STERNE
A Sentimental Journey
Tristram Shandy
ROBERT LOUIS STEVENSON
Kidnapped
Treasure Island
TOM STOPPARD
Professional Foul
Rosencrantz and Guildenstern are Dead
JONATHAN SWIFT
Gulliver's Travels
JOHN MILLINGTON SYNGE
The Playboy of the Western World
TENNYSON
Selected Poems
W. M. THACKERAY
Vanity Fair
DYLAN THOMAS
Under Milk Wood
FLORA THOMPSON
Lark Rise to Candleford
J. R. R. TOLKIEN
The Hobbit
ANTHONY TROLLOPE
Barchester Towers
MARK TWAIN
Huckleberry Finn
Tom Sawyer
JOHN VANBRUGH
The Relapse
VIRGIL
The Aeneid
VOLTAIRE
Candide
KEITH WATERHOUSE
Billy Liar
EVELYN WAUGH
Decline and Fall
JOHN WEBSTER
The Duchess of Malfi
H. G. WELLS
The History of Mr Polly
The Invisible Man
The War of the Worlds
OSCAR WILDE
The Importance of Being Earnest
THORNTON WILDER
Our Town
TENNESSEE WILLIAMS
The Glass Menagerie
VIRGINIA WOOLF
Mrs Dalloway
To the Lighthouse
WILLIAM WORDSWORTH
Selected Poems
WILLIAM WYCHERLEY
The Country Wife
W. B. YEATS
Selected Poems